CW01662611

How to use this book

Follow the advice, in italics, given for you on each page.
Support the children as they read the text that is shaded in cream.
***Praise** the children at every step!*

Detailed guidance is provided in the Read Write Inc. Phonics Handbook

9 reading activities

Children:

Practise reading the speed sounds.

Read the green, red and challenge words for the story.

Listen as you read the introduction.

Discuss the vocabulary check with you.

Read the story.

Re-read the story and discuss the 'questions to talk about'.

Read the story with fluency and expression.

Answer the questions to 'read and answer'.

Practise reading the speed words.

Speed sounds

Vowels *Say the sounds in and out of order.*

a	e	i	o	u	ay	ee	igh	ow
	ea				a-e	ea	i-e	o-e
					a	e	i	oa
					ai	y	y	o
					aigh			

oo	oo	ar	or	air	ir	ou	oy	ire	ear
u-e			oor	are	ur	ow	oi		
ue			ore		er				
ew			aw						

*Each box contains one sound but sometimes more than one grapheme. Focus graphemes are **circled**.*

Green words

Read in Fred Talk (pure sounds).

why knock straight voice quite bowl slow low those

spoke hope home toad oak road cloak throat roast

toast loaf coat Joan

Read in syllables.

a\`gain my\`self a\`live prin\`cess pal\`ace dinn\`er a\`fraid bed\`time

un\`kind be\`low pill\`ow

a\`float pett\`i\`coat slow\`coach coal-black oat\`cake

Read the root word first and then with the ending.

sail → sailing
happy → happiest
hope → hoping
groan → groaning

bounce → bouncing
marry → married
croak → croaky → croaked
foam → foaming

turn → turned
boast → boasted
moan → moaning

Red words

father one watch should there come

said who anyone whole water

Challenge words

pretty loathsome

Toad

Introduction

Do you sometimes promise to do something and then wish you hadn't? What do you do – keep your promise anyway or try to get out of it?

Princess Joan is playing in her garden one day when she drops her ball into the lake. A croaky toad offers to return it to her. In exchange he wants to eat from her plate, drink from her cup and sleep in her bed. Joan agrees and as soon as she has the ball back, she runs off.

What will the toad do?

Story written by Gill Munton
Illustrated by Tim Archbold

Vocabulary check

Discuss the meaning (as used in the story) after the children have read each word.

	definition:	sentence/phrase:
boasted	*bragged, showed off*	*She was very pretty and her father boasted about her good looks.*
roaming	*wandering, walking*	*I was roaming round the palace grounds.*
shadowy	*dark and deep*	*I watched it sink below the shadowy water.*
croaky	*rough*	*Then a croaky voice spoke to me.*
jeered	*sneered, crowed*	*'Slowcoach!' I jeered.*
gnome	*fantasy creature*	*I was turned into a toad by a gnome.*

Punctuation to note in this story:

1. Capital letters to start sentences and full stops to end sentences

2. Capital letters for names

3. Exclamation marks to show anger, shock and surprise

4. 'Wait and see' dots...

5. Speech marks

6. Apostrophes to show contractions: shouldn't wouldn't

Toad

Princess Joan lived in a palace by a lake. She was very pretty, and her father the king often boasted about her good looks.

This is Joan's story.

One day, I was roaming round the palace grounds, bouncing my ball amongst the oak trees. I went down the narrow road to the lake. I watched the sailing boats, and then I began throwing the ball into the air and catching it again.

But the ball fell into the lake.

Cross with myself, I watched it sink below the shadowy water.

Then a voice spoke to me – a croaky voice, quite close by:

"What's wrong, Princess Joan?

You woke me up, with your moaning and groaning!"

It was a toad!

A loathsome, yellow-brown toad,

afloat on a bit of wood.

I told him what had happened.

"I will get your ball back," he croaked.

"But what will you *give me*?"

"My clothes, my cloak, my petticoat, the bows in my hair ...?"

"I don't want those!" croaked the toad.

"But if you will let me eat from your bowl, drink from your mug, and sleep on your pillow -

I will be the happiest toad alive!"

I stroked his knobbly throat, and pretended to agree.

(Why should a princess want to live with an ugly old toad?)

The toad dived into the lake, and swam back with the ball.

I grabbed it, and ran home.

The toad couldn't keep up.

"Slowcoach!" I jeered.

At dinner time, there was a knock on the door.

It was the toad!

"I've come for what you owe me," he said.

I was afraid, and told my father the story.

"You must keep your promise!" he said.

So the toad *did* eat from my bowl – ugh! –

roast beef, toast, oatcakes and a whole loaf of bread!

He *did* drink from my mug – sweet, foaming cocoa.

Then the toad said, "It's bedtime now.
Pick me up, Joan, and let me sleep on your pillow!"

This was too much! I began to weep.

But my father was angry now.
"Always be kind to someone who has helped you!" he bellowed.
"Even if it's only a toad!"

Sobbing, I picked up the toad and ran to my room.
I dropped the toad on my pillow …

and straight away, he was turned into a prince!
A handsome prince, with coal-black hair and a velvet coat.

He bowed low, and said, "I was turned into a toad by a wicked gnome. You have set me free, Joan. And now I hope you will be my wife!"

So we were married, and we now live happily together.

But I will never again be unkind to anyone – not even to a toad.

Questions to talk about

Re-read the page. Read the question to the children. Tell them whether it is a **FIND IT** *question or* **PROVE IT** *question.*

FIND IT

✓ *Turn to the page*

✓ *Read the question*

✓ *Find the answer*

PROVE IT

✓ *Turn to the page*

✓ *Read the question*

✓ *Find your evidence*

✓ *Explain why*

Page 9:	PROVE IT	*Why is the beginning of this page written in italics?*
Page 10:	PROVE IT	*What was Princess Joan moaning about?*
Page 11:	PROVE IT	*Do you think the toad is clever? Why? What would you ask for?*
Page 12:	PROVE IT	*How does the princess try to trick the toad? How do you think the toad felt?*
Page 13:	PROVE IT	*Why do you think the King makes Princess Joan stick to her promise?*
Page 14:	PROVE IT	*Why is Princess Joan crying?*
Page 15:	PROVE IT	*Would you marry Princess Joan?*

Questions to read and answer

(Children complete without your help.)

1. How did Princess Joan lose her ball?

2. What did the toad look like?

3. Why did the toad agree to get the ball?

4. Why was the King cross with Princess Joan?

5. What happened to the toad when Joan dropped him on her pillow?

Speed words

Children practise reading the words across the rows, down the columns and in and out of order clearly and quickly.

myself	bouncing	bedtime	someone	happiest
palace	toast	road	boats	moaning
groaning	croaked	watched	should	couldn't
anyone	there	father	through	doesn't